Usborne

Jungle
Magic Painting
Book

Illustrated by
Federica Iossa

Designed by Brenda Cole

Try painting me!

Dip the brush
into water, then brush it
across the black patterns
and lines within each
shape to see the paint
magically appear.

To stop water
from seeping through
to the next page, unfold
the flap at the back of
the book and place it
under the page you're
about to work on.